Telekinesis Bible

Magic Quest, Volume 3

Gideon Crusader

Published by Gideon Crusader, 2022.

While every precaution has been taken in the preparation of this book, the publisher assumes no responsibility for errors or omissions, or for damages resulting from the use of the information contained herein.

TELEKINESIS BIBLE

First edition. November 13, 2022.

Copyright © 2022 Gideon Crusader.

ISBN: 979-8215618844

Written by Gideon Crusader.

Also by Gideon Crusader

Magic Quest
A Codex on Creating a Magical Phantom
Prosperity Magic for Money & Wealth
Telekinesis Bible

Table of Contents

For Maegan and Frater Z.

Introduction

Magic Quest: Telekinesis Bible is a comprehensive occult manual that discusses the magical art of telekinesis. What is telekinesis? It is the magical art of moving objects with your mind. In any practice of magic, your mind is your most powerful weapon. By harnessing the powers of the mind, you can create wonders. Telekinesis is not a new method. It has been in existence for centuries. However, among the many seekers of this power, only a few are truly able to learn it.

Magic Quest: Telekinesis Bible will not just teach you the theoretical part of telekinesis, but you will also learn its actual practices, so that you can try and see it for yourself. Interestingly, telekinesis is not really difficult to do. If you can devote enough time and effort, even by just practicing as little as an hour every day, then you can learn this ancient practice. It is also worth noting that telekinesis may be considered as a complete magical system in and of itself. As such, there are magical practitioners who focus solely on this practice alone. The reason for this is that there are other practices involved in the practice of telekinesis, especially if you truly embrace this craft sincerely.

Anyone can learn and do telekinesis—yes, even you. Some people make the mistake of thinking that they could not learn telekinesis because they are not special or that they are not gifted. But, it must be clarified that you do not need to be special or be gifted with any extraordinary power to be able to do telekinesis. As long as you have a mind (which you have) and the power to imagine (which is also an inherent ability as a human being), then you can learn to do telekinesis.

Telekinesis is really an interesting and wonderful magical practice. However, do not think that it is all about just moving objects with the mind. Indeed, telekinesis is known for such a feat, but its practices can be diverse, which necessarily includes the practice of meditation and even the development of one's spiritual life.

Are you ready to embark on a magical journey that will have real and genuine manifestation to the point that it would affect physical objects? Are you ready to unleash the powers within you and move objects with your mind? If yes, then let me now welcome you into this magical universe of telekinesis.

Let us begin...

What is Telekinesis?

Telekinesis is the psychic power and ability to move physical objects with the mind. It is considered a complete magical system. It should be emphasized that even before you can move objects with the mind, it would necessarily mean developing other skills and abilities. The actual power to move objects is just the final result or a mere manifestation of the power and spiritual development that you have gained.

Telekinesis is a learnable magical skill. You do not need to be gifted with any special ability before you can learn it. Telekinesis is for all. So, from now on, never think that you are not good enough for it. Telekinesis is simply something that you need to learn and practice. It cannot be learned just overnight, which makes it very much worth learning since being able to do it only makes it even more precious and valuable.

Telekinesis is also referred to as *psychokinesis* or simply *PK*. Now, psychokinesis has been categorized into two: micro PK and macro PK. Macro PK is how most people view what telekinesis is all about, which is the actual moving of objects with the mind. For example, with macro PK, you can move a pen or a ball with your mind. Micro PK is something that is a bit more subtle. It is the ability to influence or control probabilities. For example, you can influence a coin flip to make one side appear with a much higher probability than the actual fair probability that a coin would have if without any use of magic. In any case, just remember that both macro PK and micro PK both refer to one magical and psychic art known as *Telekinesis*.

Telekinesis has existed for centuries. Throughout history, there have been some leading figures in its practice, such as Nina Kuragina, Blavatsky, and even Uri Geller. Unfortunately, there have been some issues whether Uri Geller would count as a legitimate practitioner. Nevertheless, he still captured the attention and interest of the world. There are, of course, many other practitioners who have succeeded in its practice; but, it should be noted that true practitioners of the magical arts do not broadcast their skills. It is strongly suggested that you do the same.

The practice of telekinesis will allow you to deepen your spiritual life and enhance your overall magical skills and abilities. It can even be said that telekinesis is a way of life, as long as you embrace its practice with sincerity and devotion.

Unlike other systems of magic, telekinesis is much more flexible. You are not expected to follow the rules and principles strictly. Instead, you are given much leeway and options to make changes and modifications in accordance with your own personal preference. You are free to exercise creative expression.

Still, the best and only way to understand what telekinesis is all about is through actual experience by actually practicing the teachings and techniques.

Before you jump into the actual practices, it is important to first have the right state of mind, for all true magic starts and ends in the mind. If the mind is not sound, you could not expect to have any real progress and positive results even if you follow the procedure by the letter. Always remember that in the practice of magic, which includes the practice of telekinesis, your mind is your most powerful and important weapon. Therefore, it is important to take good care of your mental state, and this leads us to our next subject: meditation.

<u>*Quick Review*</u>

- What is telekinesis?

- What is the best way to learn telekinesis?

- What is the difference between macro and micro PK?

Meditation Practice

The practice of meditation is very important in the practice of magic, especially in the art of meditation. If you are serious about attaining any real progress, then you should definitely prioritize the regular practice of meditation. As a basic rule in the magical arts, one should meditate at least twice daily. You do not need to learn all the meditation techniques out there because all meditation techniques lead to one and the same path, and that is the path of illumination and spiritual enlightenment. It is also worth noting that the practice of meditation will naturally and effectively develop your overall magical skills and abilities.

The good news is that meditation is actually very easy to do. In fact, it is more about not doing anything than having to do something. When you meditate, always remember that it is the time for you to be calm and still. It is not the time to worry about things or think about anything. The modern world is so designed that we are often bombarded with so many things and pressures of life. Be very careful not to fall into this trap. Instead, you must learn to keep your mind quiet and still. It is in stillness where great power can be harnessed.

A common mistake in meditation is to allow yourself to be bombarded with so many thoughts. It should be clear that the moment of meditation is a moment of calm and stillness. Although you may be tempted to entertain the thoughts that appear in the mind, you must be careful not to allow these thoughts to misdirect you. Instead, use the moment to focus on the actual meditation practice itself. You must free the mind, and only then can you free the soul. Having said that, the best and only way to understand what meditation is all about is through actual practice. Let us now begin with your first actual lesson on meditation. The meditation technique that you are about to learn is known as the *meditation on the breath*. It is a classic of meditation. The steps are as follows:

Assume a comfortable position and relax. Close your eyes and do not think about anything. Breathe through your nose. Now, gently focus on your breath. You must focus only on the breath in exclusion of all other thoughts. Only the breath must exist in the mind. Know that he who meditates on the breath is actually meditating on life, for breath is life.

If thoughts continue to arise in the mind, simply ignore them. If your mind wanders off, just bring it ever so gently back to your breath. Be one with your breath. Breath is life.

Continue this meditation for as long as you like. Soon enough, you will experience being in a deep state of mind. Just continue with the meditation. Nothing must exist in the mind but the breath. Breathe and let go.

At any time that you want to end this meditation, simply bring your awareness ever so gently back to your physical body, slowly move your fingers and toes, and gently open your eyes with a smile.

It cannot be overemphasized that the practice of meditation is very important. Be sure to make this a daily priority in your life, and you will never go wrong with your magical practice. In fact, there are advanced practitioners out there who do no other practices but only this simple meditation. Never underestimate the power of this meditation, for its power actually lies in its simplicity. Breathe, relax, and let go.

Another meditation technique that you should know is the use of a mantra or a power word. The mantra or power word will be your point of focus in the meditation instead of the breath. The steps are the same as the meditation that we have just discussed; but this time, instead of focusing on the breath, you will be focusing on your power word. It can be any word or sound. Many practitioners use the mantra *OM* (also pronounced as *AUM*). You may also use a different word that you like. One that I would recommend is the name of *Jesus*. Just keep saying your power word and focus on it. In the beginning, you may have to chant or whisper it; but as you gain more experience and as you reach a deeper state of mind, you will notice that you no longer have to say it physically for you will be able to hear it as some kind of an inner voice. Once you reach this stage, you can stop physically saying your power word and simply focus on the inner voice that is chanting it.

Now that you know how to meditate, all that is left is for you to do is to put it into continuous practice. Do not be discouraged if nothing seems to happen on your first several attempts. Just keep on practicing, and you will surely reap the many benefits of meditation soon.

Quick Review

- What is meditation?

- How many times should you meditate every day?

- Is meditation difficult?

The Magical Mindset

The practice of meditation will also allow you to reach the state of mind that is referred to as the magical mindset. It is the mindset that is optimized for magical work, which is also the state of mind that is necessary for the effective practice of telekinesis.

The magical mindset is the mind that is well established in the teachings and foundations of magic. It is the mind that is still and calm. It is the level of mind that has faith and believes what it is doing. It is a mind that is unshakable.

The practice of meditation will allow you to achieve this state of mind. The more that your level of mind comes close to the optimum magical mindset, the easier that you will be able to do telekinesis successfully.

There are those who teach that you can attain the magical mindset overnight by using a certain technique, but such a view is erroneous and merely illusory because the real magical mindset is something that comes about only through continuous practice of magical techniques, as well as the application of magical teachings.

There is no shortcut to achieving the magical mindset. You simply have to live the true magical life, and only then will the magical mindset unfold on its own. No secrets, and definitely no shortcuts. Do not worry, this does not mean that you need to attain the high level of magical mindset first before you can successfully do telekinesis. You can still get positive results even without actually attaining the real level of magical mindset. Still, the closer you get to the optimum magical mindset, the more that you can harness the power of telekinesis easily and more effectively.

Therefore, instead of focusing on how you can attain the magical mindset, a better approach is to simply put the magical teachings into actual practice by truly living a magical life—and the magical mindset will come naturally.

Quick Review

- What is the magical mindset?

- How do you acquire the magical mindset?

Mind Over Matter & Energy

It should be realized that mind is, indeed, over matter. But, how does this happen? What is the hidden science behind it? It is a long-standing teaching in magic that all things are made of magical energy. This energy goes far beyond what conventional science believes as to what energy is all about. This energy in magic is of pure and divine origin. It is inside us and all around us. It is the energy that pervades the whole universe.

All things, visible and invisible, are made of energy. It then follows that by learning how to control this energy, you can also gain control over all things. Telekinesis is also the manipulation of this energy. The key to manipulating this energy is with the mind. There is an ancient teaching among the alchemists of the Old Age that says, "The All is Mind; the Universe is Mental." Indeed, this is a true and genuine teaching that is now even considered as one of the universal laws of nature, as well as a law of magic. Truly, the mind is your most powerful weapon as a magus.

How can the mind be that powerful? There are various views on this matter, and some of them even go so far as to contradict one another. However, it appears that the most convincing school of thought is that our mind is always connected to the Great Mind, also known as the One True Source of All Things, or simply God. This connection that we have with the Great Mind is what makes the potential of our little mind infinite.

The mind is often active in the astral plane, which is the realm of the spirits, thoughts, and the imagination. However, this does not mean that it cannot affect the physical plane. You must understand that the astral dimension and the physical realm are co-existing with each other. And, everything that happens in the physical world has its connection in the astral dimension. In fact, everything that has any form of manifestation in the physical has already long manifested in the astral dimension. As you can see, it can be viewed that the physical world is a mere fruit or creation of the astral matrix.

A practitioner of telekinesis must understand that matter is subject to the mind. From a magical perspective, matter is just an accumulation of magical energy. As such, the mind has complete dominion and control over matter, and this can be done through the practice of telekinesis.

When the mind is still and quiet, it can easily direct the flow of energy. This is another reason why the practice of meditation is considered a must in the art of telekinesis. To have real success, you must still your mind. Indeed, there is so much power in stillness.

Magic starts and ends in the mind. Spells and rituals also originate and even happen in the mind. There are two schools of thought that are relevant to this matter. One school of thought believes that physical objects may hold power. Another school of thought, and one that is more relevant to telekinesis, posits that physical objects do not by themselves have any power except only the mind that holds it. Simply put, it is only the mind that creates the power. As you can see, your mind is very powerful.

However, it is your duty to be able to direct it in a magical way and in a way that is most effective. Telekinesis teaches a person to harness the mind in a magical manner. This is another reason why telekinesis is considered a complete magical system in and of itself. Indeed, if you dedicate yourself to the practice of telekinesis, you will surely be a real magus/witch.

Quick Review

- What is magical energy?

- How can the mind be so powerful?

- Can the mind affect the physical plane?

Matchstick Exercise

This is a classic exercise in the practice of telekinesis. For this exercise, you will just be needing matches. The idea here is to light the match and be able to control the flame. The reason why we use a match instead of a candle is that the energy of a newly-lit match is much easier to control than the flame of a candle. The steps are as follows:

Be comfortable and relax. Light the match and look at the flame. Focus gently on the flame. Nothing must exist in your mind but the flame. As you focus on the flame, an instant connection will be naturally made between you and the flame. Once you feel this connection, just maintain it. The more that you are connected to the flame, the more easily that you will be able to control it.

Now, the next step takes some willpower and the use of the imagination. Your objective is to make the flame jump out of the matchstick. To do this, use your will to make the flame move and jump off the stick. As you are doing this, imagine the flame already doing it. Imagine the flame actually jumping off the stick. When imagination and willpower come together, great and magical things can happen. Continue practicing this daily and as often as you can. You will soon achieve positive results if you practice regularly.

Quick Review

- Why use a matchstick instead of a candle?

- How do you make a connection with the flame?

Candle Flame Exercise

This is the technique that I strongly recommend, especially for beginners. For this exercise, you are just going to use a lighted candle. Simply prepare the candle and sit right in front of it. You may also do this exercise even while standing or even while lying down. Still, the sitting position is most ideal.

Just relax and clear your mind. Stare at the flame of the candle and clear your mind. Do not think about anything. By simply focusing on the flame, you will naturally create a connection to it. Just relax as you get more connected to the flame.

Now, you are going to make the flame of the candle move by bending it to one side. To do this, you are going to use your willpower and imagination. Imagine the flame of the candle bending to the right (or to whatever direction that you want it to bend to). As you are doing this, use your willpower to actually command the physical flame to move. Keep doing this over and over again until the physical flame actually moves in the direction that you want.

You are not limited to just making the flame of the candle bend to a certain direction. If you want, you can also control the size of the flame. You can make it smaller and bigger. The method is the same: use your will and imagination.

It should be noted that there is a third element that is necessary in telekinesis, and that is having oneness with the object that you intend to move. The more that you feel connected and at one with the object, the more easily that you will be able to move it with your mind.

Feel free to take full control over the flame of the candle. Unlike the previous technique, this one is much more convenient to practice with. Be sure to take advantage of this exercise, and you will surely be able to develop your telekinetic skills.

<u>Quick Review</u>

- How do you make the flame of a candle bend to a particular direction?

- Can telekinesis control the size of a candle flame?

On Oneness

What does it really mean to be one with the object that you intend to move? And, just how are you going to go about it? This connection of oneness is something that goes about by itself. By focusing on the object, a connection is made instantly. It is the connection of your soul with the object that you want to move.

An important point to observe is to be open. The soul will make its connection on its own. You do not need to force it. In fact, forcing it would be counterproductive to your efforts. Remember the universal principle that energy follows thought. By focusing gently on the object, a thought connection is created between you and the object. This connection is made of energy. And, this is easily achieved simply by gently focusing on the object. As you can see, everything happens on its own automatically.

A common mistake is to try to force the connection of oneness. True oneness is not forced. It is something that can only happen when the flow of energy between two things is smooth and harmonious. This is something that cannot happen when you use force. Instead of using force, just be open and relax. When you are open and relaxed, energy will flow more smoothly. You must also realize that you are already naturally magical, so you do not really need to exert extra effort. You just have to bring the magic within you into manifestation, and this is something that you can do without using force. Instead, be gentle and be open to the energy of magic to unfold in your life.

Having a deep connection or oneness with the object that you want to move usually takes practice. The key here is simply to keep on practicing. The more that you practice, the more that you will improve and develop your skills.

Quick Review

- What is oneness in magic?

- How can you develop oneness in telekinesis?

Levitate

This technique is a simple and effective technique that you can use to levitate a light and small object, such as a feather. With enough practice, you may also be able to use this technique to levitate other light objects, such as a pen or a piece of paper. It uses the willpower and the magical technique known as *forcecraft* wherein certain formula words are chanted to manipulate energy and cause the levitation that is desired.

This technique uses the following words of power: *Stiff as a board, light as a feather.* The steps are as follows:

Be comfortable and relax. Hold the object, preferably a feather, pen, or any other small and light object by placing it flat on your palms. Focus lightly on the object and begin to chant your power words: *Stiff as a board, light as a feather.*

As you are doing this, use your willpower to command the object to levitate. This is done just by mere force of will. However, it must be noted that this is not a kind of force that is imposing or something that is akin to abusing something; but rather, it is a gentle and harmonious exercise of willpower. Think of it as leading someone in a dance. If you direct the energy of the object in this manner, you will notice that you are more able to manipulate the energy effectively. This is something that you can apply to any other magical practices that involve the manipulation of magical energy.

As you are doing the aforesaid steps, the object may start to rise (levitate) from your hands. When this happens, it is important that you remain calm. Having a high emotion or feeling excited will only prevent the magic from continuously working. Just keep going with the technique to make the object levitate even higher.

A common mistake that beginners make when they do this is that they ask themselves questions while in the process, such as, "Is it working?" or "Is it levitating already?" and so on. Remember that the actual practice itself is not the right time to ask questions. The time to ask questions is after the practice, but not during. During the actual practice, the only focus must be on the magical work at hand.

<u>*Quick Review*</u>

- What are the words of power to cast levitation?

- Should you ask questions while engaged in magical work?

- Why is it that you cannot be too excited during the actual practice of telekinesis itself?

Pure Willpower Technique

If you are the type of person who likes to impose their will or who feels like they have a very strong willpower, then this approach might be suitable for you. This technique is all about the use of willpower. It is contrary to the main teaching because this technique is not about harmony or oneness; but rather, it is all about the pure exercise of the will, in whatever way, and for any purpose—as long as you achieve the objective that you desire. In fact, this technique is so imposing that it uses force through the power of the will. After all, magic is an art, and there can be exceptions to the general rules. Having said that, here are the steps:

Be comfortable and relax. Choose an object that you want to move. It is good to start with a fairly light object, such as a pen or a crumpled piece of paper. Another good option is a balloon that is placed on a table or any other flat surface. Now, look at the object and focus on it. It should be noted that this is not a gentle approach, but this technique finds its power in making strong commands through the pure exercise of the will. As you are focusing on the object, imagine that it is already moving in the way that you want it to move. As you are doing this, command it to move by actually talking to it, saying, "Move!"

Feel free to impose your will and force the object to move with the powerful force of your will. This technique may not be for everyone, but there are practitioners who prefer using this approach. Just give it a try and see how it works for you.

If you think that you do not have a strong will, then the practice of meditation would be very helpful yet again. Meditation practice is one of the best methods to develop and strengthen willpower, which is another reason why you should definitely prioritize your meditation practice.

Quick Review

- Is there an exception to the general rule that one should not use force in the practice of telekinesis?

- If yes, what is the exception?

Energy Wave

This technique uses a wave of energy to move an object. The energy wave is projected from your hand. The projected energy will push the object, thereby causing it to be pushed forward; hence, making it move. If you are fond of direct energy manipulation, then you may find this technique of interest. I know some magicians and witches who could not do any form of telekinesis until they learned about this approach. If you are having a hard time doing telekinesis, then this is a technique that is definitely worth trying. Having said that, the steps are as follows:

It is good to use this technique on a balloon. However, if a balloon is not available, you can still use this technique on any light object that can easily be pushed forward, such as a ball or the flame of a candle.

Next, hold out your hand. You can use either hand. It is the hand where energy will be projected to push an object. Most people like to use their dominant hand for this purpose. Imagine magical energy shooting out from your hand, and then press the ray of energy out toward the object that you want to move. Take note that you are now using your very own personal energy. Keep pouring and pressing energy against the object until it moves.

You can also use the energy from the universe instead of your own personal energy. This is to avoid draining yourself of energy. So that you will not be drained, you can easily tap and harness the energy all around you. To do this, imagine magical energy all around you. I usually tell my students to visualize it as white light. See and feel that this magical energy is being drawn to and is being absorbed by your hand. Continue to charge your hand with energy. You should be able to feel the build up of energy in your hand. Once you sense a powerful accumulation of energy, you can then use that energy to push the object instead of your own personal energy.

<u>*Quick Review*</u>

- How can you prevent yourself from being drained of your personal energy?

- Is it possible to cause telekinesis using direct energy manipulation?

Spoon Bending

Spoon bending is a classic of magick. It is one of the best demonstrations of telekinetic power. Spoon bending is not limited to spoons. You can also use a fork or any other hard object that is capable of being bent. However, when you practice telekinesis, know that you are bending the object only with the mind. The physical actions of the hands may be added, but you must not use so much force. It is allowed to touch the spin or even manually flex it with the hand, but you must not apply as much physical force, the primary force must still come from your mind.

There are two methods of spoon bending: one that has physical assistance and one where no physical assistance at all is involved. Needless to say, the latter is much more difficult and is usually done only by advanced practitioners. Having said that, let us now proceed to the actual steps:

For this exercise, you will be needing a spoon. Hold the spoon with one hand and keep the other hand free. You may hold the spoon in any way that you want. I like to hold it by the handle as I position it vertically. Now, just relax and focus gently on the spoon. Feel the energy of the spoon. You should be able to sense it as you are holding it with your hand. Make the spoon a part of yourself. Let its energy merge with yours. You may visualize the energy of the spoon flowing through your hands, thereby combining it with your very own energy. Soon enough, you may feel that the spoon has already become a part of you.

Using your other hand, hold the end of the spoon and also feel the energy. Be one with the spoon. Once you feel that you are one with the spoon, thereby making it a part of yourself, will it to bend with your mind as if you were moving it as a mere part of your body. At the same time, simply fold or bend it with your hand. However, in doing so, the hand (or both hands) should not apply so much force but must assist only in the bending of the spoon. If done correctly, the spoon should be easily folded or bent as if it were very soft.

Another way of bending the spoon is with the mind only. This is reserved for higher levels, but it is something that you can always try. The principle is exactly the same as the one that we have just discussed; however, at the moment of bending or folding the spoon, you should not use your other hand to bend the spoon. In fact, you should not use your hands at all. The only hand that you will use is the hand that is holding the spoon, and its purpose is only to hold the spoon and nothing more. Hence, you will be bending the spoon solely with your mind. For this technique, I suggest that you apply your visualization and use your willpower. Imagine the spoon already bending repeatedly and then will it to actually happen once you have connected to the spoon and established oneness with it.

Spoon bending is an excellent exercise that can significantly develop your telekinetic ability. However, just like anything worth learning, this technique usually takes time and practice. The key is to keep on practicing, and you will surely get better and better in time.

<u>*Quick Review*</u>

- Is spoon bending limited only to the use of a spoon?

- Can you use actual physical action when you do spoon bending?

Micro PK

Micro PK is the telekinetic ability to control or influence randomness, such as the roll of the dice or the flip of a coin. This is usually demonstrated through a series of trials. If you are into gambling, then you might find this practice of interest.

For this exercise, you will be using a coin or a die. You are going to influence or control it in such a way that a certain must appear more frequently than the others. To simplify, let us use an ordinary coin. The steps are as follows:

Be comfortable and relax. Choose which side of the coin you want to appear. Let us say that you pick heads. Now, imagine flipping the coin and that it keeps coming up as heads. Use this visualization together with your willpower. As you are doing this, this time, actually flip the actual physical coin and know that it shall be just as you have imagined it. Continue to apply the basic principles like visualization and the application of willpower. Continue this for about 100 flips/trials. After 100 rolls (which is 100%), check if the side that you want to appear has appeared the most. If done correctly, the side that you want to appear must appear significantly more than the other side of the coin.

<u>*Quick Review*</u>

- What is micro PK?

- In micro PK, is it necessary to always get the right result?

Paper Telekinesis

This is one of my most favorite telekinesis exercises. It is also one of the easiest to do. For this exercise, you are going to use a paper. It is strongly recommended to use parchment paper since it is sensitive to energy. You can easily attain positive results with parchment paper. However, if this is not possible, any ordinary paper will do. I have also tried it with regular paper money with good results. However, using other kinds of paper rather than parchment paper can be more challenging. Therefore, if you are a beginner, try to get parchment paper.

This is a really interesting technique that has a pretty nice visual effect. Let us now discuss the steps:

Tear the paper to about the size of your palm. It does not have to be a perfect cut/tear. Next, place the paper on the palm of your hand, palm facing upward. You are going to draw and accumulate energy in your palm that is holding the paper. To do this, imagine magical energy around you. You may visualize it as pure white light. See and feel that you are drawing energy from all around you, and have the energy accumulate in your hand that is holding the paper.

Continue to add more and more energy in your hand. Take note that you are not charging the paper with energy, but it is your hand that is being charged with energy. Continue to charge your hand with energy as much as you can and for as long as you want. As you are doing this, observe the paper on your palm. Is it moving? The point here is that the paper will react to the high amount of energy that is being accumulated in your hand, thereby causing the paper to move.

Master tip: Before you do this exercise, you can fold the paper about twice to put creases on it. This will make the movement of the paper even more apparent. Another thing that I like to do is to place the paper on someone else's palm. You should do this only after you have already charged the paper with energy (after you expose it to your magically-charged hand). Once you gain even more experience, you can place the paper on a table; and, even without the use of your hand, you should be able to make it move by directly sending energy to it.

So, what causes the paper to move? In this exercise, the paper reacts to the accumulated energy in your hand, causing it to move naturally. If you do not put creases on the paper, the paper will most likely bend, and even pop upward. If you put creases on it, the paper will take like a folding motion before it pops.

Although parchment paper is best, it should be noted that this technique also works on any kind of paper as long as it is easily foldable. I have tried doing it with regular paper and with paper bills with good results. Still, if you want to be able to do it easily and see some really nice visuals, then parchment paper would be best.

This is an interesting technique that has a really nice visual effect. Moreover, regular practice of this technique will also significantly develop your skills in the direct manipulation of energy.

<u>*Quick Review*</u>

- What type of paper is best for the exercise that we have just described?

- What causes the paper to move?

- What is the benefit of putting creases on the paper?

Make Your Own

You are also free to come up with your own techniques for telekinesis. Know that this book is only a key that opens the door that leads to so many paths and adventures of magic. Magic is an art, so feel free to express yourself and make absolute use of your creativity.

You are also free to make adjustments to the teachings in this book in accordance with your personal preferences. In fact, you are hereby encouraged to develop your own techniques and make your own magical discoveries. After all, the practice of magic is both a science and an art.

Having your own technique is usually something that happens naturally. Normally, people tend to make some adjustments here and there to help them incorporate a certain technique into their own practices. By doing so, and after a series of tweaking and changes, a "new" technique is created. There are also others who intentionally create techniques that are completely unique in all aspects. The important thing to note is to satisfy the scientific requirements, and then you are free to have full exercise of the artistic aspect of telekinesis.

Do not let this book or any other book create limitations in your mind. You are infinite as long as you believe it. Do not entertain doubts. Keep your mind positive, and keep your enthusiasm to learn telekinesis alive. It is also easier to have success in telekinesis when you are having fun than when you are too serious, or worse, if you are disappointed. When your heart is filled with positive energy, then it will be significantly much easier to do telekinesis because a soul that is charged with positive energy will allow the energies of the universe to flow smoothly and naturally, thereby making it possible for great and wonderful magic to happen.

<u>Quick Review</u>

- Is it okay to make your own telekinesis techniques?

- Is magic also considered an art?

Best Practices

Let us now discuss the essential best practices that you may observe in the practice of telekinesis. If combined together, these practices may significantly help increase your rate of success:

Meditation is key

The practice of meditation cannot be overemphasized. Meditation is a natural way to develop your overall psychic and magical faculties. Be sure to prioritize it and make it a part of your daily magical and spiritual practices.

When you meditate, do not be like the others who force something to happen. Meditation is a moment of deep relaxation and stillness. It is the moment of letting go of everything—and this includes letting go even of your expectations. Keep the mind still and quiet by following the technique that you are using. Be still, relax, and let go of everything.

Be calm and relax

When you practice telekinesis, you should train your mind to be calm and relax at all times, especially when you are engaged in magical practice. When it comes to calming and relaxing the mind, the practice of meditation will once again be very helpful. You should also avoid getting too excited. You must keep your mind under your control at all times. This usually takes practice, but it is nonetheless doable. In fact, as a magical practitioner, this is something that you must learn as early as possible. You will need this not only in the practice of telekinesis, but also in all other magical practices.

Strengthen your willpower

By now, you should already know that the willpower plays an important role in the magical arts, especially in the practice of telekinesis. The following exercise will help you develop your willpower. It is a form of meditation that includes concentration. For this exercise, you will need a small and simple object, such as a pen or anything simple. Here are the steps:

Be comfortable and relax. Place the object in front of you and gently focus on it. Keep your mind open. If thoughts arise in the mind, ignore them. Just focus on the object. Nothing must exist in the mind but the object. This is how you exercise and develop your willpower.

Of course, every magical act develops the willpower. The important thing is to have a specific will, and that you must pursue that course of action regardless of any distractions and challenges.

Work with small and light objects

If you are just starting to learn telekinesis, it is good to work with small and light objects. When you work with a light object, the mind will more easily be convinced that you can be able to move it as compared with having to move a heavy object. It also takes more energy to move a heavier object. Therefore, if you are starting out, it is strongly encouraged to work and experiment only on small and light objects, such as a feather, flame of a candle, pen, and paper, among others.

Reflect

It is a good practice to make it a habit to stop and reflect every now and then. This also helps to ensure that you are not being misdirected or manipulated by the modern world. You should look within yourself and examine your life, as well as the things that you do and the thoughts that you keep in your mind.

Speaking about the mind, from now on, be very careful with the thoughts that you keep and entertain in your mind. Never forget that your mind is your most powerful weapon. As such, you should keep it strong, healthy, and magical. As a basic rule, you must only entertain positive thoughts, and you ought to get rid of and/or let go of all negative thoughts as soon as possible. Be sure to include this in your examination of the self, and always be very honest with yourself.

Have a positive mindset

It is always a good idea to keep a positive mindset. When the mind is sound and well, the more that it will be able to work magically. You may notice that when you are not in a good mood, it seems to be more difficult to do any form of telekinesis. In fact, you may find that during such moments, it is impossible to do any kind of magic at all. From now on, take very good care of your mind. Never forget that your mind is your most powerful weapon. Keep it pure and magical all the time, and never let the pressures and tricks of this modern world corrupt your mind.

Faith

It is important to have faith in what you do. You must know that your magic is more than good enough, and that you are more than good enough. In the beginning, this may be difficult, but it is something that you can work on and develop over time. The key here is to gain more experience. Now, the only way to gain more experience is by actually engaging in actual practice, and you ought to do so regularly. The more experience you have, the more confidence you will also have as your skills develop over time. Soon enough, you will have enough faith to move objects—perhaps even the divine faith to move a mountain.

Since we are already talking about faith, let me just share with you something beautiful—and that is the faith in Jesus Christ. If you are able to gain this faith, then everything will be possible for you. Indeed, so many witches and wizards these days are turning to Christ for a deeper spirituality. If religion disappoints you, do not worry because you do not need to follow a religion. In fact, you do not even need to be a part of any religion to get to know Christ and follow Him.

Love

Why do you want to learn the ancient art of telekinesis? How will your loved ones benefit from it? If you have love in your heart, then you will be more able to wield a strong force—for love is the strongest force in the universe. Look within you and find this love, and then let this love inspire you whenever you do a magical work. This applies in telekinesis, as well as in any magical practice that you may find yourself engaged in.

<u>Quick Review</u>

- Name up to three best practices that you can observe to increase your chances of success.

A Message

The practice of telekinesis is not a difficult system. In fact, it is very straightforward. If you just give it enough time and effort, then it really has so much to offer to you. The best way of practice is to turn the teachings and techniques into a way of life. This way, you will be living a truly magical life. After all, true magic is meant to be lived and experienced on a deep and personal level.

Once you go deep into this practice, you will see that telekinesis actually means so much more than moving objects with the mind. Such a feat can be viewed as a mere consequence or fruit of practicing telekinesis.

Just like any other art, telekinesis is something that you get good at over time through repeated practice. The key is to keep practicing, preferably every day. The more that you spend time and effort to learn this magical art, the more that you will improve. In the beginning, you will most likely encounter some failures along the way. However, do not lose heart. Instead, keep yourself motivated, and always do your best.

I would also like to take this opportunity to share the call to Christ. Many magical practitioners are now turning to Jesus Christ for a much deeper form of spirituality. This does not mean that you have to join a church. After all, Jesus is for all. It is strongly suggested that you try to get to know Christ on your own. A good start is by reading the Bible, especially the Book of Matthew. In fact, you can start with the Book of Matthew, which also happens to be the first book in the New Testament. This way, you can get to know Christ, as well as His divine teachings.

Last but not least, enjoy every step of the journey. After all, the magical path has no end. Keep learning and keep discovering new and exciting things. Enjoy life as a true magical practitioner. Be happy, be true, be you, and be free.

THE END

The Author

www.charlzdelacruz.com

Password to enter the private page: ANGEL912

Don't miss out!

Visit the website below and you can sign up to receive emails whenever Gideon Crusader publishes a new book. There's no charge and no obligation.

https://books2read.com/r/B-A-VRRV-FGUCC

BOOKS 2 READ

Connecting independent readers to independent writers.

Did you love *Telekinesis Bible*? Then you should read *A Codex on Creating a Magical Phantom*[1] by Gideon Crusader!

[2]

Magic Quest: A Codex on Creating a Magical Phantom is a direct and easy to understand manual that teaches the art of creating the so-called magical phantom. What is a magical phantom? It is a creation of the magus, and it serves him in whatever purpose he desires. This magical craft has existed for centuries. A thorough research on the history of magic will reveal that this ancient art has been practiced by witches and wizards for centuries. To this day, true practitioners of magic employ magical phantoms to

---

1. https://books2read.com/u/3nXklK

2. https://books2read.com/u/3nXklK

make their will manifest on all planes of existence, as well as to have a strong and trustworthy magical ally.

Magic Quest: A Codex on Creating a Magical Phantom reveals the essential teachings and knowledge that you need to start creating your very own magical phantom. By the time you finish reading this codex, you will have unlocked the secrets behind this magical mystery.

Magic Quest: A Codex on Creating a Magical Phantom will not only teach you how to create the legendary magical phantom, but it will also develop your overall magical faculties. If you are willing to put in the time and effort to learn this magical technique, then you will be able to cast real and powerful magic. Indeed, this kind of magic is learnable as long as you know the right instructions. After gaining the right knowledge, it is up to you to put the teachings into actual and continuous practice toward mastery of the technique.

Are you ready to embark on a journey of real magic? If yes, then let me know welcome you into this magical universe where you shall awaken the power that lies within and where your desires shall be the very laws that govern the universe. Welcome into this world of eternal magic.

Also by Gideon Crusader

Magic Quest
A Codex on Creating a Magical Phantom
Prosperity Magic for Money & Wealth
Telekinesis Bible